51st Annual Meeting of the Association for Computational Linguistics (ACL 2013)

Tutorial Abstracts

Sofia, Bulgaria
4-9 August 2013

ISBN: 978-1-62748-978-2

Printed from e-media with permission by:

Curran Associates, Inc.
57 Morehouse Lane
Red Hook, NY 12571

Some format issues inherent in the e-media version may also appear in this print version.

Printed by Curran Associates, Inc. (2013)

For permission requests, please contact the Association for Computational Linguistics at the address below.

Association for Computational Linguistics
209 N. Eighth Street
Stroudsburg, Pennsylvania 18360

Phone: 1-570-476-8006
Fax: 1-570-476-0860

acl@aclweb.org

Additional copies of this publication are available from:

Curran Associates, Inc.
57 Morehouse Lane
Red Hook, NY 12571 USA
Phone: 845-758-0400
Fax: 845-758-2634
Email: curran@proceedings.com
Web: www.proceedings.com

Introduction

This volume contains the abstracts of the ACL 2013 tutorials. We received 25 high-quality proposals, and we were faced with the challenging task to make a suitable selection. We applied the following criteria for evaluation: appropriateness, technical fit, novelty, potential interest, presenters, and experience. In the end we accepted seven tutorials. Six of these are organized as half-day tutorials, and one is given as a full-day tutorial.

We are very grateful to Roberto Navigli (publication chair), Svetla Koeva (local chair), Hinrich Schuetze (general chair), Michael Strube (the ACL 2012 tutorial chair), Stefano Faralli (publication), and of course Priscilla Rasmussen, for various kinds of help, advice and assistence offered during the process of putting the tutorial programme and materials together. Finally, we would like to thank the tutorial presenters for the time and effort in preparing and presenting the tutorials.

We hope you will enjoy the tutorials!

ACL 2013 Tutorial Chairs

Johan Bos (University of Groningen)
Keith Hall (Google Research)

Tutorial Chairs:

Johan Bos, University of Groningen
Keith Hall, Google Research

Table of Contents

Visual Features for Linguists: Basic image analysis techniques for multimodally-curious NLPers

Elia Bruni
University of Trento
elia.bruni@unitn.it

Marco Baroni
University of Trento
marco.baroni@unitn.it

Description

Features automatically extracted from images constitute a new and rich source of semantic knowledge that can complement information extracted from text. The convergence between vision- and text-based information can be exploited in scenarios where the two modalities must be combined to solve a target task (e.g., generating verbal descriptions of images, or finding the right images to illustrate a story). However, the potential applications for integrated visual features go beyond mixed-media scenarios: Because of their complementary nature with respect to language, visual features might provide perceptually grounded semantic information that can be exploited in purely linguistic domains.

The tutorial will first introduce basic techniques to encode image contents in terms of low-level features, such as the widely adopted SIFT descriptors. We will then show how these low-level descriptors are used to induce more abstract features, focusing on the well-established bags-of-visual-words method to represent images, but also briefly introducing more recent developments, that include capturing spatial information with pyramid representations, soft visual word clustering via Fisher encoding and attribute-based image representation. Next, we will discuss some example applications, and we will conclude with a brief practical illustration of visual feature extraction using a software package we developed.

The tutorial is addressed to computational linguists without any background in computer vision. It provides enough background material to understand the vision-and-language literature and the less technical articles on image analysis. After the tutorial, the participants should also be able to autonomously incorporate visual features in their NLP pipelines using off-the-shelf tools.

Outline

1. Why image analysis?
   - The grounding problem
   - Multimodal datasets (Pascal, SUN, ImageNet and ESP-Game)
2. Extraction of low-level features from images
   - Challenges (viewpoint, illumination, scale, occlusion, etc.)
   - Feature detectors
   - Feature descriptors
3. Visual words for higher-level representation of visual information
   - Constructing a vocabulary of visual words
   - Classic Bags-of-visual-words representation
   - Recent advances
   - Computer vision applications: Object recognition and emotion analysis
4. Going multimodal: Example applications of visual features in NLP
   - Generating image descriptions
   - Semantic relatedness
   - Modeling selectional preference

Semantic Parsing with Combinatory Categorial Grammars

Yoav Artzi, Nicholas FitzGerald and **Luke Zettlemoyer**
Computer Science & Engineering
University of Washington
Seattle, WA 98195
{yoav,nfitz,lsz}@cs.washington.edu

1 Abstract

Semantic parsers map natural language sentences to formal representations of their underlying meaning. Building accurate semantic parsers without prohibitive engineering costs is a long-standing, open research problem.

The tutorial will describe general principles for building semantic parsers. The presentation will be divided into two main parts: modeling and learning. The modeling section will include best practices for grammar design and choice of semantic representation. The discussion will be guided by examples from several domains. To illustrate the choices to be made and show how they can be approached within a real-life representation language, we will use λ-calculus meaning representations. In the learning part, we will describe a unified approach for learning Combinatory Categorial Grammar (CCG) semantic parsers, that induces both a CCG lexicon and the parameters of a parsing model. The approach learns from data with labeled meaning representations, as well as from more easily gathered weak supervision. It also enables *grounded* learning where the semantic parser is used in an interactive environment, for example to read and execute instructions.

The ideas we will discuss are widely applicable. The semantic modeling approach, while implemented in λ-calculus, could be applied to many other formal languages. Similarly, the algorithms for inducing CCGs focus on tasks that are formalism independent, learning the meaning of words and estimating parsing parameters. No prior knowledge of CCGs is required. The tutorial will be backed by implementation and experiments in the University of Washington Semantic Parsing Framework (UW SPF).[1]

[1] http://yoavartzi.com/spf

2 Outline

1. Introduction to CCGs
2. Modeling
   (a) Questions for database queries
   (b) Plurality and determiner resolution in grounded applications
   (c) Event semantics and imperatives in instructional language
3. Learning
   (a) A unified learning algorithm
   (b) Learning with supervised data
      i. Lexical induction with templates
      ii. Unification-based learning
   (c) Weakly supervised learning without labeled meaning representations

3 Instructors

Yoav Artzi is a Ph.D. candidate in the Computer Science & Engineering department at the University of Washington. His research studies the acquisition of grounded natural language understanding within interactive systems. His work focuses on modeling semantic representations and designing weakly supervised learning algorithms. He is a recipient of the 2012 Yahoo KSC award.

Nicholas FitzGerald is a Ph.D. student at the University of Washington. His research interests are grounded natural language understanding and generation. He is a recipient of an Intel Science and Technology Center Fellowship and an NSERC Postgraduate Scholarship.

Luke Zettlemoyer is an Assistant Professor in the Computer Science & Engineering department at the University of Washington. His research interests are in the intersections of natural language processing, machine learning and decision making under uncertainty. Honors include best paper awards at UAI 2005 and ACL 2009, selection to the DARPA CSSG, and an NSF CAREER Award.

Decipherment

Kevin Knight
USC/ISI
4676 Admiralty Way
Marina del Rey CA 90292
knight@isi.edu

Abstract

The first natural language processing systems had a straightforward goal: decipher coded messages sent by the enemy. This tutorial explores connections between early decipherment research and today's NLP work. We cover classic military and diplomatic ciphers, automatic decipherment algorithms, unsolved ciphers, language translation as decipherment, and analyzing ancient writing as decipherment.

1 Tutorial Overview

The first natural language processing systems had a straightforward goal: decipher coded messages sent by the enemy. Sixty years later, we have many more applications, including web search, question answering, summarization, speech recognition, and language translation. This tutorial explores connections between early decipherment research and today's NLP work. We find that many ideas from the earlier era have become core to the field, while others still remain to be picked up and developed.

We first cover classic military and diplomatic cipher types, including complex substitution ciphers implemented in the first electro-mechanical encryption machines. We look at mathematical tools (language recognition, frequency counting, smoothing) developed to decrypt such ciphers on proto-computers. We show algorithms and extensive empirical results for solving different types of ciphers, and we show the role of algorithms in recent decipherments of historical documents.

We then look at how foreign language can be viewed as a code for English, a concept developed by Alan Turing and Warren Weaver. We describe recently published work on building automatic translation systems from non-parallel data. We also demonstrate how some of the same algorithmic tools can be applied to natural language tasks like part-of-speech tagging and word alignment.

Turning back to historical ciphers, we explore a number of unsolved ciphers, giving results of initial computer experiments on several of them. Finally, we look briefly at writing as a way to encipher phoneme sequences, covering ancient scripts and modern applications.

2 Outline

1. Classical military/diplomatic ciphers (15 minutes)
   - 60 cipher types (ACA)
   - Ciphers vs. codes
   - Enigma cipher: the mother of natural language processing
     - computer analysis of text
     - language recognition
     - Good-Turing smoothing
2. Foreign language as a code (10 minutes)
   - Alan Turing's "Thinking Machines"
   - Warren Weaver's Memorandum
3. Automatic decipherment (55 minutes)
   - Cipher type detection
   - Substitution ciphers (simple, homophonic, polyalphabetic, etc)
     - plaintext language recognition
       * how much plaintext knowledge is needed

        * index of coincidence, unicity distance, and other measures
    - navigating a difficult search space
        * frequencies of letters and words
        * pattern words and cribs
        * EM, ILP, Bayesian models, sampling
    - recent decipherments
        * Jefferson cipher, Copiale cipher, civil war ciphers, naval Enigma
- Application to part-of-speech tagging, word alignment
- Application to machine translation without parallel text
- Parallel development of cryptography and translation
- Recently released NSA internal newsletter (1974-1997)

4. *** Break *** (30 minutes)

5. Unsolved ciphers (40 minutes)
    - Zodiac 340 (1969), including computational work
    - Voynich Manuscript (early 1400s), including computational work
    - Beale (1885)
    - Dorabella (1897)
    - Taman Shud (1948)
    - Kryptos (1990), including computational work
    - McCormick (1999)
    - Shoeboxes in attics: DuPonceau journal, Finnerana, SYP, Mopse, diptych

6. Writing as a code (20 minutes)
    - Does writing encode ideas, or does it encode phonemes?
    - Ancient script decipherment
        - Egyptian hieroglyphs
        - Linear B
        - Mayan glyphs
        - Ugaritic, including computational work
        - Chinese Nüshu, including computational work
    - Automatic phonetic decipherment
    - Application to transliteration

7. Undeciphered writing systems (15 minutes)
    - Indus Valley Script (3300BC)
    - Linear A (1900BC)
    - Phaistos disc (1700BC?)
    - Rongorongo (1800s?)

8. Conclusion and further questions (15 minutes)

3 About the Presenter

Kevin Knight is a Senior Research Scientist and Fellow at the Information Sciences Institute of the University of Southern California (USC), and a Research Professor in USC's Computer Science Department. He received a PhD in computer science from Carnegie Mellon University and a bachelor's degree from Harvard University. Professor Knight's research interests include natural language processing, machine translation, automata theory, and decipherment. In 2001, he co-founded Language Weaver, Inc., and in 2011, he served as President of the Association for Computational Linguistics. Dr. Knight has taught computer science courses at USC for more than fifteen years and co-authored the widely adopted textbook *Artificial Intelligence*.

Exploiting Social Media for Natural Language Processing: Bridging the Gap between Language-centric and Real-world Applications

Simone Paolo Ponzetto
Research Group Data and Web Science
University of Mannheim
Mannheim, Germany
simone@informatik.uni-mannheim.de

Andrea Zielinski
Fraunhofer IOSB
Fraunhoferstraße 1
Karlsruhe, Germany
andrea.zielinski@iosb.fraunhofer.de

Introduction

Social media like Twitter and micro-blogs provide a goldmine of text, shallow markup annotations and network structure. These information sources can all be exploited together in order to automatically acquire vast amounts of up-to-date, wide-coverage structured knowledge. This knowledge, in turn, can be used to measure the pulse of a variety of social phenomena like political events, activism and stock prices, as well as to detect emerging events such as natural disasters (earthquakes, tsunami, etc.).

The main purpose of this tutorial is to introduce social media as a resource to the Natural Language Processing (NLP) community both from a scientific and an application-oriented perspective. To this end, we focus on micro-blogs such as Twitter, and show how it can be successfully mined to perform complex NLP tasks such as the identification of events, topics and trends. Furthermore, this information can be used to build high-end socially intelligent applications that tap the wisdom of the crowd on a large scale, thus successfully bridging the gap between computational text analysis and real-world, mission-critical applications such as financial forecasting and natural crisis management.

Tutorial Outline

1. Social media and the wisdom of the crowd. We review the resources which will be the focus of the tutorial, i.e. Twitter and micro-blogging in general, and present their most prominent and distinguishing aspects (Kwak et al., 2010; Gouws et al., 2011), namely: (i) instant short-text messaging, including its specific linguistic characteristics (e.g., non-standard spelling, shortenings, logograms, etc.) and other features – i.e., mentions (@), hashtags (#), shortened URLs, etc.; (ii) a dynamic network structure where users are highly inter-connected and author profile information is provided along with other metadata. We introduce these properties by highlighting the different trade-offs related to resources of this kind, as well as their comparison with alternative data publishing platforms – for instance, highly unstructured text vs. rich network structure, semi-structured metadata tagging (like hashtags) vs. fully-structured linked open data, etc.

2. Analyzing and extracting structured information from social media. We provide an in-depth overview of contributions aimed at tapping the wealth of information found within Twitter and other micro-blogs. We first show how social media can be used for many different NLP tasks, ranging from pre-processing tasks like PoS tagging (Gimpel et al., 2011) and Named Entity Recognition (Ritter et al., 2011) through high-end discourse (Ritter et al., 2010) and information extraction applications like event detection (Popescu et al., 2011; Ritter et al., 2012) and topic tracking (Lin et al., 2011). We then focus on novel tasks and challenges opened up by social media such as *geoparsing*, which aims to predict the location (including its geographic coordinates) of a message or user based on his posts (Gelernter and Mushegian, 2011; Han et al., 2012), and methods to automatically establish the credibility of user-generated content by making use of contextual and metadata features (Castillo et al., 2011).

3. Exploiting social media for real-world applications: trend detection, social sensing and crisis management. We present methods to detect emerging events and breaking news from social media (Mathioudakis et al., 2010; Petrović et al., 2010, *inter alia*). Thanks to their highly dynamic environment and continuously updated content, in fact, micro-blogs and social networks are capable of providing real-time information for a wide variety of different social phenomena, including consumer confidence and presidential job approval polls (O'Connor et al., 2010), as well as stock market prices (Bollen et al., 2011; Ruiz et al., 2012). We focus in particular on applications that use social media for health surveillance in order to monitor, for instance, flu epidemics (Aramaki et al., 2011), as well as crisis management systems that leverage them for tracking natural disasters like earthquakes (Sakaki et al., 2010; Neubig et al., 2011) and tsunami (Zielinski and Bürgel, 2012; Zielinski et al., 2013).

References

Eiji Aramaki, Sachiko Maskawa, and Mizuki Morita. 2011. Twitter catches the flu: detecting influenza epidemics using Twitter. In *Proc. of EMNLP-11*, pages 1568–1576.

Johan Bollen, Huina Mao, and Xiaojun Zeng. 2011. Twitter mood predicts the stock market. *Journal of Computational Science*, 2(1):1–8.

Carlos Castillo, Marcelo Mendoza, and Barbara Poblete. 2011. Information credibility on Twitter. In *Proc of WWW-11*, pages 675–684.

Judith Gelernter and Nikolai Mushegian. 2011. Geoparsing messages from microtext. *Transactions in GIS*, 15(6):753–773.

Kevin Gimpel, Nathan Schneider, Brendan O'Connor, Dipanjan Das, Daniel Mills, Jacob Eisenstein, Michael Heilman, Dani Yogatama, Jeffrey Flanigan, and Noah A. Smith. 2011. Part-of-speech tagging for Twitter: Annotation, features, and experiments. In *Proc. of ACL-11*, pages 42–47.

Stephan Gouws, Donald Metzler, Congxing Cai, and Eduard Hovy. 2011. Contextual bearing on linguistic variation in social media. In *Proceedings of the Workshop on Language in Social Media (LSM 2011)*, pages 20–29.

Bo Han, Paul Cook, and Timothy Baldwin. 2012. Geolocation prediction in social media data by finding location indicative words. In *Proc. of COLING-12*, pages 1045–1062.

Haewoon Kwak, Changhyun Lee, Hosung Park, and Sue Moon. 2010. What is Twitter, a social network or a news media? In *Proc of WWW-10*, pages 591–600.

Jimmy Lin, Rion Snow, and William Morgan. 2011. Smoothing techniques for adaptive online language models: topic tracking in tweet streams. In *Proc. of KDD-11*, pages 422–429.

Michael Mathioudakis, Nick Koudas, and Peter Marbach. 2010. Early online identification of attention gathering items in social media. In *Proc. of WSDM-10*, pages 301–310.

Graham Neubig, Yuichiroh Matsubayashi, Masato Hagiwara, and Koji Murakami. 2011. Safety information mining – what can NLP do in a disaster –. In *Proceedings of IJCNLP-11*, pages 965–973.

Brendan O'Connor, Ramnath Balasubramanyan, Bryan R. Routledge, and Noah A. Smith. 2010. From tweets to polls: linking text sentiment to public opinion time series. In *Proc. of ICWSM-10*, pages 122–129.

Saša Petrović, Miles Osborne, and Victor Lavrenko. 2010. Streaming first story detection with application to Twitter. In *Proc. of NAACL-10*, pages 181–189.

Ana-Maria Popescu, Marco Pennacchiotti, and Deepa Paranjpe. 2011. Extracting events and event descriptions from Twitter. In *Comp. Vol. to Proc. of WWW-11*, pages 105–106.

Alan Ritter, Colin Cherry, and Bill Dolan. 2010. Unsupervised modeling of Twitter conversations. In *Proc. of NAACL-10*, pages 172–180.

Alan Ritter, Sam Clark, Mausam, and Oren Etzioni. 2011. Named entity recognition in tweets: an experimental study. In *Proc. of EMNLP-11*, pages 1524–1534.

Alan Ritter, Mausam, Oren Etzioni, and Sam Clark. 2012. Open domain event extraction from Twitter. In *Proc. of KDD-12*, pages 1104–1112.

Eduardo J. Ruiz, Vagelis Hristidis, Carlos Castillo, Aristides Gionis, and Alejandro Jaimes. 2012. Correlating financial time series with micro-blogging activity. In *Proc. of WSDM-12*, pages 513–522.

Takeshi Sakaki, Makoto Okazaki, and Yutaka Matsuo. 2010. Earthquake shakes Twitter users: real-time event detection by social sensors. In *Proc. of WWW-10*, pages 851–860.

Andrea Zielinski and Ulrich Bürgel. 2012. Multilingual analysis of Twitter news in support of mass emergency events. In *Proc. of ISCRAM-12*.

Andrea Zielinski, Stuart E. Middleton, Laurissa Tokarchuk, and Xinyue Wang. 2013. Social-media text mining and network analysis to support decision support for natural crisis management. In *Proc. of ISCRAM-13*.

Robust Automated Natural Language Processing with Multiword Expressions and Collocations

Valia Kordoni and Markus Egg
Humboldt-Universität zu Berlin (Germany)
kordonie@anglistik.hu-berlin.de,
markus.egg@anglistik.hu-berlin.de

1 Introduction

This tutorial aims to provide attendees with a clear notion of the linguistic and distributional characteristics of *multiword expressions* (MWEs), their relevance for robust automated natural language processing and language technology, what methods and resources are available to support their use, and what more could be done in the future. Our target audience are researchers and practitioners in language technology, not necessarily experts in MWEs, who are interested in tasks that involve or could benefit from considering MWEs as a pervasive phenomenon in human language and communication.

2 Topic Overview

Multiword expressions (MWEs) like *break down*, *bus stop* and *make ends meet*, are expressions consisting of two or more lexical units that correspond to some conventional way of saying things (Sag et al., 2001). They range over linguistic constructions such as fixed phrases (*per se, by and large*), noun compounds (*telephone booth, cable car*), compound verbs (*give a presentation*), idioms (*a frog in the throat, kill some time*), etc. They are also widely known as collocations, for the frequent co-occurrence of their components (Manning and Schütze, 2001).

From a natural language processing perspective, the interest in MWEs comes from the very important role they play forming a large part of human language, which involves the use of linguistic routines or prefabricated sequences in any kind of text or speech, from the terminology of a specific domain (*parietal cortex, substantia nigra, splice up*) to the more colloquial vocabulary (*freak out, make out, mess up*) and the language of the social media (*hash tag, fail whale, blackbird pie*). New MWEs are constantly being introduced in the language (*cloud services, social networking site, security apps*), and knowing how they are used reflects the ability to successfully understand and generate language.

While easily mastered by native speakers, their treatment and interpretation involves considerable effort for computational systems (and non-native speakers), due to their idiosyncratic, flexible and heterogeneous nature (Rayson et al., 2010; Ramisch et al., to appear). First of all, there is the task of identifying whether a given sequence of words is an MWE or not (e.g. *give a gift* vs. *a presentation*) (Pecina, 2008; Green et al., 2013; Seretan, 2012). For a given MWE, there is also the problem of determining whether it forms a compositional (*take away the dishes*), semi-idiomatic (*boil up the beans*) or idiomatic combination (*roll up your sleeves*) (Kim and Nakov, 2011; Shutova et al., 2013). Furthermore, MWEs may also be polysemous: *bring up* as carrying (*bring up the bags*), raising (*bring up the children*) and mentioning (*bring up the subject*). Unfortunately, solutions that are successfully employed for treating similar problems in the context of simplex works may not be adequate for MWEs, given the complex interactions between their component words (e.g. the idiomatic use of *spill* in *spilling beans* as revealing secrets vs. its literal usage in *spilling lentils*).

3 Content Overview

This tutorial consists of four parts. Part I starts with a thorough introduction to different types of MWEs and collocations, their linguistic dimensions (idiomaticity, syntactic and semantic fixedness, specificity, etc.), as well as their statistical characteristics (variability, recurrence, association, etc.). This part concludes with an overview of linguistic and psycholinguistic theories of MWEs to date.

For MWEs to be useful for language technology, they must be recognisable automatically.

Hence, Part II surveys computational approaches for MWEs recognition, both manually-authored approaches and using machine learning techniques, and for modeling syntactic and semantic variability. We will also review token identification and disambiguation of MWEs in context (e.g. *bus stop* in *Does the bus stop here?* vs. *The bus stop is here*) and methods for the automatic detection of the degree of compositionality of MWEs and their interpretation. Part II finishes with a discussion of evaluation for MWE tasks.

Part III of the tutorial describes resources made available for a wide range of languages as well as MWE-related multi-level annotation platforms and examples of where MWEs treatment can contribute to language technology tasks and applications such as parsing, word sense disambiguation, machine translation, information extraction and information retrieval. Part IV concludes with a list of future possibilities and open challenges in the computational treatment of MWEs in current NLP models and techniques.

4 Tutorial Outline

1. PART I – General overview:
   (a) Introduction
   (b) Types and examples of MWEs and collocations
   (c) Linguistic dimensions of MWEs: idiomaticity, syntactic and semantic fixedness, specificity, etc.
   (d) Statistical dimensions of MWEs: variability, recurrence, association, etc.
   (e) Linguistic and psycholinguistic theories of MWEs
2. PART II – Computational methods
   (a) Recognising the elements of MWEs: type identification
   (b) Recognising how elements of MWEs are combined: syntactic and semantic variability
   (c) Token identification and disambiguation of MWEs
   (d) Compositionality and Interpretation of MWEs
   (e) Evaluation of MWE tasks
3. PART III – Resources, tasks and applications:
   (a) MWEs in resources: corpora, lexica and ontologies (e.g. Wordnet and Genia)
   (b) Tools for MWE identification and annotation (e.g. NSP, mwetoolkit, UCS and jMWE)
   (c) MWEs and Collocations in NLP tasks: Parsing, POS-tagging, Word Sense Disambiguation (WSD)
   (d) MWes and Collocations in Language Technology applications: Information Retrieval (IR), Information Extraction (IE), Machine Translation (MT)
4. PART IV – Future challenges and open problems

References

Spence Green, Marie-Catherine de Marneffe, and Christopher D. Manning. 2013. Parsing models for identifying multiword expressions. *Computational Linguistics*, 39(1):195–227.

Su Nam Kim and Preslav Nakov. 2011. Large-scale noun compound interpretation using bootstrapping and the web as a corpus. In *EMNLP*, pages 648–658.

Ioannis Korkontzelos and Suresh Manandhar. 2010. Can recognising multiword expressions improve shallow parsing? In *Human Language Technologies: The 2010 Annual Conference of the North American Chapter of the Association for Computational Linguistics*, pages 636–644, Los Angeles, California, June. Association for Computational Linguistics.

Christopher D. Manning and Hinrich Schütze. 2001. *Foundations of statistical natural language processing*. MIT Press.

Pavel Pecina. 2008. A machine learning approach to multiword expression extraction. In Nicole Grégoire, Stefan Evert, and Brigitte Krenn, editors, *Proceedings of the LREC Workshop Towards a Shared Task for Multiword Expressions (MWE 2008)*, pages 54–57.

Carlos Ramisch, Paulo Schreiner, Marco Idiart, and Aline Villavicencio. 2008. An evaluation of methods for the extraction of multiword expressions. In Nicole Grégoire, Stefan Evert, and Brigitte Krenn, editors, *Proceedings of the LREC Workshop Towards a Shared Task for Multiword Expressions (MWE 2008)*, pages 50–53.

Carlos Ramisch, Aline Villavicencio, and Valia Kordoni. to appear. *Special Issue on Multiword Expressions*. ACM TSLP.

Paul Rayson, Scott Songlin Piao, Serge Sharoff, Stefan Evert, and Begoña Villada Moirón. 2010. Multiword expressions: hard going or plain sailing? *Language Resources and Evaluation*, 44(1-2):1–5.

Ivan A. Sag, Timothy Baldwin, Francis Bond, Ann Copestake, and Dan Flickinger. 2001. Multiword expressions: A pain in the neck for NLP. In *Proc. of the 3rd International Conference on Intelligent Text Processing and Computational Linguistics (CICLing-2002*, pages 1–15.

Violeta Seretan. 2012. *Syntax-Based Collocation Extraction*, volume 44, Text, Speech and Language Technology. Springer.

Ekaterina Shutova, Simone Teufel, and Anna Korhonen. 2013. Statistical metaphor processing. *Comput. Linguist.*, 39(2):301–353, June.

Aline Villavicencio, Francis Bond, Anna Korhonen, and Diana McCarthy. 2005. Introduction to the special issue on multiword expressions: Having a crack at a hard nut. *Computer Speech & Language*, 19(4):365–377.

Aline Villavicencio, Valia Kordoni, Yi Zhang, Marco Idiart, and Carlos Ramisch. 2007. Validation and evaluation of automatically acquired multiword expressions for grammar engineering. In *Proceedings of the 2007 Joint Conference on Empirical Methods in Natural Language Processing and Computational Natural Language Learning (EMNLP-CoNLL)*, pages 1034–1043, Prague, Czech Republic, June. Association for Computational Linguistics.

Variational Inference for Structured NLP Models

David Burkett and **Dan Klein**
Computer Science Division
University of California, Berkeley
{dburkett,klein}@cs.berkeley.edu

Description

Historically, key breakthroughs in structured NLP models, such as chain CRFs or PCFGs, have relied on imposing careful constraints on the locality of features in order to permit efficient dynamic programming for computing expectations or finding the highest-scoring structures. However, as modern structured models become more complex and seek to incorporate longer-range features, it is more and more often the case that performing exact inference is impossible (or at least impractical) and it is necessary to resort to some sort of approximation technique, such as beam search, pruning, or sampling. In the NLP community, one increasingly popular approach is the use of variational methods for computing approximate distributions.

The goal of the tutorial is to provide an introduction to variational methods for approximate inference, particularly mean field approximation and belief propagation. The intuition behind the mathematical derivation of variational methods is fairly simple: instead of trying to directly compute the distribution of interest, first consider some efficiently computable approximation of the original inference problem, then find the solution of the approximate inference problem that minimizes the distance to the true distribution. Though the full derivations can be somewhat tedious, the resulting procedures are quite straightforward, and typically consist of an iterative process of individually updating specific components of the model, conditioned on the rest. Although we will provide some theoretical background, the main goal of the tutorial is to provide a concrete procedural guide to using these approximate inference techniques, illustrated with detailed walkthroughs of examples from recent NLP literature.

Once both variational inference procedures have been described in detail, we'll provide a summary comparison of the two, along with some intuition about which approach is appropriate when. We'll also provide a guide to further exploration of the topic, briefly discussing other variational techniques, such as expectation propagation and convex relaxations, but concentrating mainly on providing pointers to additional resources for those who wish to learn more.

Outline

1. Structured Models and Factor Graphs
    - Factor graph notation
    - Example structured NLP models
    - Inference
2. Mean Field
    - Warmup (iterated conditional modes)
    - Mean field procedure
    - Derivation of mean field update
    - Example
3. Structured Mean Field
    - Structured approximation
    - Computing structured updates
    - Example: Joint parsing and alignment
4. Belief Propagation
    - Intro
    - Messages and beliefs
    - Loopy BP
5. Structured Belief Propagation
    - Warmup (efficient products for messages)
    - Example: Word alignment
    - Example: Dependency parsing
6. Wrap-Up
    - Mean field vs BP
    - Other approximation techniques

Presenter Bios

David Burkett is a postdoctoral researcher in the Computer Science Division at the University of California, Berkeley. The main focus of his research is on modeling syntactic agreement in bilingual corpora. His interests are diverse, though, and he has worked on parsing, phrase alignment, language evolution, coreference resolution, and even video game AI. He has worked as an instructional assistant for multiple AI courses at Berkeley and won multiple Outstanding Graduate Student Instructor awards.

Dan Klein is an Associate Professor of Computer Science at the University of California, Berkeley. His research includes many areas of statistical natural language processing, including grammar induction, parsing, machine translation, information extraction, document summarization, historical linguistics, and speech recognition. His academic awards include a Sloan Fellowship, a Microsoft Faculty Fellowship, an NSF CAREER Award, the ACM Grace Murray Hopper Award, Best Paper Awards at ACL, EMNLP and NAACL, and the UC Berkeley Distinguished Teaching Award.

The mathematics of language learning

András Kornai
Computer and Automation Research Institute
Hungarian Academy of Sciences
andras@kornai.com

Gerald Penn
Department of Computer Science
University of Toronto
gpenn@cs.utoronto.edu

James Rogers
Computer Science Department
Earlham College
jrogers@cs.earlham.edu

Anssi Yli-Jyrä
Department of Modern Languages
University of Helsinki
anssi.yli-jyra@helsinki.fi

Over the past decade, attention has gradually shifted from the estimation of parameters to the learning of linguistic structure (for a survey see Smith 2011). The Mathematics of Language (MOL) SIG put together this tutorial, composed of three lectures, to highlight some alternative learning paradigms in speech, syntax, and semantics in the hopes of accelerating this trend.

Compounding the enormous variety of formal models one may consider is the bewildering range of ML techniques one may bring to bear. In addition to the surprisingly useful classical techniques inherited from multivariate statistics such as Principal Component Analysis (PCA, Pearson 1901) and Linear Discriminant Analysis (LDA, Fisher 1936), computational linguists have experimented with a broad range of neural net, nearest neighbor, maxent, genetic/evolutionary, decision tree, max margin, boost, simulated annealing, and graphical model learners. While many of these learners became standard in various domains of ML, within CL the basic HMM approach proved surprisingly resilient, and it is only very recently that deep learning techniques from neural computing are becoming competitive not just in speech, but also in OCR, paraphrase, sentiment analysis, parsing and vector-based semantic representations. The first lecture will provide a mathematical introduction to some of the fundamental techniques that lie beneath these linguistic applications of neural networks, such as: BFGS optimization, finite difference approximations of Hessians and Hessian-free optimization, contrastive divergence and variational inference.

Lecture 1: The mathematics of neural computing – *Penn*

Recent results in acoustic modeling, OCR, paraphrase, sentiment analysis, parsing and vector-based semantic representations have shown that natural language processing, like so many other corners of artificial intelligence, needs to pay more attention to neural computing.

I Gaussian Mixture Models
- Lagrange's theorem
- Stochastic gradient descent
- typical acoustic models using GMMs and HMMs

II Optimization theory
- Hessian matrices
- Broyden-Fletcher-Goldfarb-Shanno theory
- finite difference approximations of Hessians
- Hessian-free optimization
- Krylov methods

III Application: Product models
- products of Gaussians vs. GMMs
- products of "experts"
- Gibbs sampling and Markov-chain Monte Carlo
- contrastive divergence

IV Experimentation: Deep NNs for acoustic modeling
- intersecting product models with Boltzmann machines
- "generative pre-training"
- acoustic modeling with Deep Belief Networks
- why DBNs work well

V Variational inference
- variational Bayes for HMMs

In spite of the enormous progress brought by ML techniques, there remains a rather significant range of tasks where automated learners cannot yet get near human performance. One such is the unsupervised learning of word structure addressed by MorphoChallenge, another is the textual entailment task addressed by RTE.

The second lecture recasts these and similar problems in terms of learning weighted edges in a sparse graph, and presents learning techniques that seem to have some potential to better find spare finite state and near-FS models than EM. We will provide a mathematical introduction to the Minimum Description Length (MDL) paradigm and spectral learning, and relate these to the better-known techniques based on (convex) optimization and (data-oriented) memorization.

Lecture 2: Lexical structure detection – *Kornai*

While modern syntactic theory focuses almost entirely on productive, rule-like regularities with compositional semantics, the vast bulk of the information conveyed by natural language, over 85%, is encoded by improductive, irregular, and non-compositional means, primarily by lexical meaning. Morphology and the lexicon provide a rich testing ground for comparing structure learning techniques, especially as inferences need to be based on very few examples, often just one.

I Motivation

- Why study structure?
- Why study lexical structure?

II Lexical structure

- Function words, content words
- Basic vocabulary (Ogden 1930, Swadesh 1950, Yasseri et al 2012)
- Estimation style

III Formal models of lexical semantics

- Associative (Findler 1979, Dumais 2005, CVS models)
- Combinatorial (FrameNet)
- Algebraic (Kornai 2010)

IV Spectral learning

- Case frames and valency
- Spectral learning as data cleaning (Ng 2001)
- Brew and Schulte im Walde 2002 (German), Nemeskey et al (Hungarian)
- Optionality in case frames

V Models with zeros

- Relating ungrammaticality and low probability (Pereira 2000, Stefanowitsch 2006)
- Estimation errors, language distances (Kornai 1998, 2011)
- Quantization error

VI Minimum description length

- Kolmogorov complexity and universal grammar (Clark 1994)
- MDL in morphology (Goldsmith 2000, Creutz and Lagus 2002, 2005,...)
- MDL for weighted languages
- Ambiguity
- Discarding data – yes, you can!
- Collapsing categories

VII New directions

- Spectral learning of HMMs (Hsu et al 2009, 2012)
- of weighted automata (Balle and Mohri 2012)
- Feature selection, LASSO (Pajkossy 2013)
- Long Short-Term Memory (Monner and Reggia 2012)
- Representation learning (Bengio et al 2013)

Given the broad range of competing formal models such as templates in speech, PCFGs and various MCS models in syntax, logic-based and association-based models in semantics, it is somewhat surprising that the bulk of the applied work is still performed by HMMs. A particularly significant case in point is provided by PCFGs, which have not proved competitive with straight trigram models. Undergirding the practical failure of PCFGs is a more subtle theoretical problem, that the nonterminals in better PCFGs cannot be identified with the kind of nonterminal labels that grammarians assume, and conversely, PCFGs embodying some form of grammatical knowledge tend not to outperform flatly initialized models that make no use of such knowledge. A natural response to this outcome is to retrench and use less powerful formal models, and the last lecture will be spent in the *subregular* space of formal models even less powerful than finite state automata.

Lecture 3: Subregular Languages and Their Linguistic Relevance – *Rogers* and *Yli-Jyrä*

The difficulty of learning a regular or context-free language in the limit from positive data gives a motivation for studying non-Chomskyan language classes. The lecture gives an overview of the taxonomy of the most important subregular classes of languages and motivate their linguistic relevance in phonology and syntax.

I Motivation

- Some classes of (sub)regular languages
- Learning (finite descriptions of) languages
- Identification in the limit from positive data
- Lattice leaners

II Finer subregular language classes

- The dot-depth hierarchy and the local and piecewise hierarchies
- k-Local and k-Piecewise Sets

III Relevance to phonology

- Stress patterns
- Classifying subregular constraints

IV Probabilistic models of language

- Strictly Piecewise Distributions (Heinz and Rogers 2010)

V Relevance to syntax

- Beyond the inadequate right-linear grammars
- Parsing via intersection and inverse morphism

- Subregular constraints on the structure annotations
- Notions of (parameterized) locality in syntax.

The relevance of some parameterized subregular language classes is shown through machine learning and typological arguments. Typological results on a large set of languages (Heinz 2007, Heinz et al 2011) relate language types to the theory of subregular language classes.

There are finite-state approaches to syntax showing subregular properties. Although structure-assigning syntax differs from phonotactical constraints, the inadequacy of right-linear grammars does not generalize to all finite-state representations of syntax. The linguistic relevance and descriptive adequacy are discussed, in particular, in the context of intersection parsing and conjunctive representations of syntax.

Instructors

Anssi Yli-Jyrä is Academy Research Fellow of the Academy of Finland and Visiting Fellow at Clare Hall, Cambridge. His research focuses on finite-state technology in phonology, morphology and syntax. He is interested in weighted logic, dependency complexity and machine learning.

James Rogers is Professor of Computer Science at Earlham College, currently on sabbatical at the Department of Linguistics and Cognitive Science, University of Delaware. His primary research interests are in formal models of language and formal language theory, particularly model-theoretic approaches to these, and in cognitive science.

Gerald Penn teaches computer science at the University of Toronto, and is a Senior Member of the IEEE. His research interests are in spoken language processing, human-computer interaction, and mathematical linguistics.

András Kornai teaches at the Algebra Department of the Budapest Institute of Technology, and leads the HLT group at the Computer and Automation Research Institute of the Hungarian Academy of Sciences. He is interested in everything in the intersection of mathematics and linguistics. For a list of his publications see http://kornai.com/pub.html.

Online resources

Slides for the tutorial:
http://molweb.org/acl13tutorial.pdf
Bibliography:
http://molweb.org/acl13refs.pdf
Software:
http://molweb.org/acl13sw.pdf

Author Index